One Big Family, Full of Love

Michelle Gidaspova

with contributions by Anna Gidaspova

To the memory of my grandparents,

Christian and Janet Burkhart,

to my mother Paula,

and to future generations of our family,

that we may be inspired by their spirit of love.

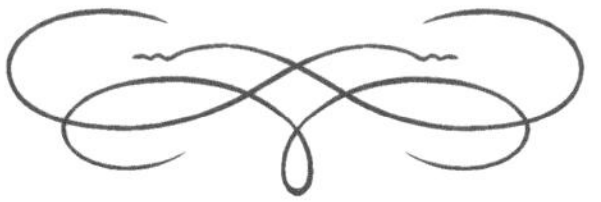

This is a story about love. It is also the story of my grandparents. You see, they knew the secret that all loving families know: the more love you give, the more you have!

God is love, and when you put your trust in Him, He will put so much love in your heart that you can't possibly hold it all in!

Chris and Janet were special people, full of love. As children, they always thanked God for what they had, even when it wasn't a lot. When they grew up and fell in love, they decided to marry. They asked God to bless their marriage, and they stayed close to Him all their lives.

Because each of them came from a very small family, together they dreamed of having a very big family. They believed that more children would bring more love. And that's just what happened!

WELCOME
to
St. Mary's

Soon Chris and Janet became a Mom and a Dad. Their 1st child was Jim. Jim was a serious child who studied hard and dreamed of becoming a rocket scientist – and one day he did!

Their 2nd child, Marianne, was born
two years later. Marianne was fun –
she loved to dance! She wore skirts
with poodles on them.

Their 3rd child, Elaine, was born two years later. Elaine loved people and knew everyone in the neighborhood.

Their 4th child, Paula, was born two years later. Paula loved people too! Together, Elaine and Paula gathered lots of children to play hopscotch and many other games outside.

Their 5th child, Fred, was born two years later. Fred loved trucks — fire trucks, dump trucks, tractor trailors… all kinds of trucks.

Their 6th child, Richard, was born two years later. Just like Fred, Richard also loved trucks! Most of all, Fred and Richard loved crashing their trucks together.

Their 7th child, Andrea, was born two years later. Andrea was a happy child. When she was two years old, though, she caught a sickness and died. This made Mom and Dad very sad, but they knew she was with God and that He knew best. Losing Andrea made them love their other children more.

Their 8th child, Chris, was born two years later. He was the only child in the family who was able to convince his parents to get a dog. He loved his puppy and named him "Midnight."

Their 9th child, Dave, was born two years later. When Dave was in school, he told his dad that girls were gross and he would never, ever, EVER get married! His dad was smart and asked him to write it down and sign it. When Dave was older and got married, Dad gave that letter to Dave's wife!

Finally, their 10th child, Tommy, was born five years later. Tommy liked playing football and baseball with his brothers, but he also spent a lot of time taking care of his Grandpa. His Grandpa had helped their family so much, and now he needed some help too.

Their Grandma and Grandpa lived upstairs. When things got hectic, Grandma was always ready with fresh cookies and a warm lap.

25

The whole family — ten kids, their parents, and their grandparents — lived in a small house on St. Joseph's Street. The girls shared one bedroom, and the boys shared the other bedroom. One year the snow was so deep, the kids sledded out the upstairs window!

With so many kids, Mom couldn't keep track of them all. She watched the youngest ones closely, and she asked the older ones to watch everyone else. Sometimes that worked, and sometimes it didn't.

But whatever happened, they always ended the day
with love.

GLORIA

Christmas was a joyful time for the family. They celebrated Jesus' birth by singing Christmas carols and giving each other gifts. And they always baked a birthday cake for Baby Jesus!

They had a lot of kids and a small car. They had a lot
of love and not a lot of money. But every summer, they
packed everyone into the car to explore a new place. They
visited the Liberty Bell in Philadelphia, the monuments
in Washington, D.C., and even the World's Fair in New
York City.

They also spent a lot of time at a cottage in the woods, during the summer when school was out. The cottage didn't have running water or an indoor toilet, but it did have a lot of nature!

Chris and Janet's children eventually grew up, had their own children, who had their own children, who had their own children, and so on. With God's help, they planted a tree of love, which still grows strong today.